# 20 Spanish Baroque

## by Gaspar Sanz
## Arranged for Uke

by Rob MacKillop

**Online Audio**    www.melbay.com/22128BCDEB

---

### AUDIO CONTENTS

---

1 2 3 4 5 6 7 8 9 0

Visit us on the Web at www.melbay.com — E-mail us at email@melbay.com

# ♫ CONTENTS ♫

# Introduction

**Gaspar Sanz** (1640 – 1710) is the most famous baroque-period guitarist. His works are tuneful and memorable, with fiery cross-rhythms and cascading scale passages. They have been arranged for orchestra by Joaquin Rodrigo (*Fantasia par un Gentilhombre*) and performed by classical guitarists and baroque guitar specialists. Sanz was born in Calanda, Spain, in 1640, and studied music, literature and divinity at the University of Salamanca. He travelled to Rome and studied the works of the great Italian guitar virtuosi. On his return to Spain he published three books of guitar music, and was appointed guitar teacher to Don Juan of Austria.

**The Baroque Guitar** could be viewed as a close relative of the **ukulele**. Indeed, the two instruments have much in common. The tuning used by Gaspar Sanz was *re-entrant*, that is, the strings did not rise in pitch from low to high, but were arranged as follows:

This five-course guitar has four pairs of strings and one single treble. The lowest note, as with the ukulele, is the third string. Sanz enjoyed playing scales in the *campanella* style, with the notes of a scale set out on different strings, sonically overlapping slightly in the style of little bells. This is a technique the ukulele excels at, and is used to good effect in these arrangements. There are many passages in Sanz's music where notes of a melody suddenly leap up or down octaves. Apparently this was acceptable, and is commonplace in other guitar publications of the period. This is helpful when arranging for the ukulele, and there are many passages here which use this practice to advantage.

The smaller four-course guitar actually had the same tuning as the ukulele, although it was largely double-strung: gG cc e'e' a'. The ukulele tuning used in this publication uses a high g for the fourth – essential for the realisation of the many campanella passages. Small guitars were common in Portugal, especially the Madeiran *machete* – which found its way in 1879 to Hawai'i, where it became known as the ukulele.

I have played Sanz's music on the baroque guitar (see robmackillop.net for videos and mp3 files) and believe much of it transfers well to the uke. It is hoped that this repertoire will bring a refreshing addition to the repertoire of the ukulele, just as the little instrument can bring a freshness to these old but lively pieces.

Rob MacKillop

# Las Hachas

Gaspar Sanz, 1674
Arr. Rob MacKillop©

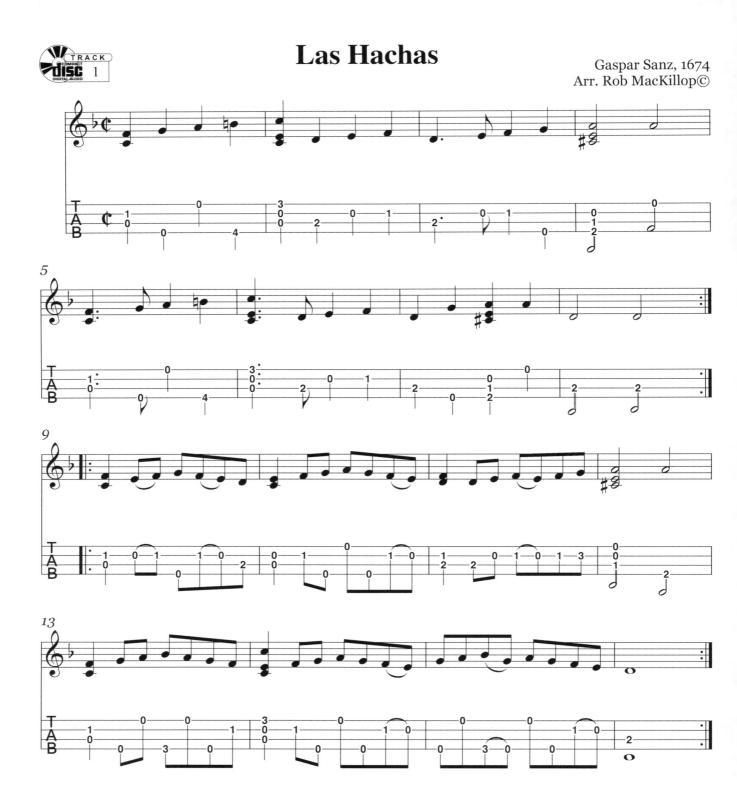

This page has been deliberately left blank

# Zarabanda

Gaspar Sanz, 1674
Arr. Rob MacKillop©

# Zarabanda Francesa (1)

Gaspar Sanz, 1674
Arr. Rob MacKillop©

# Zarabanda Francesa (2)

Gaspar Sanz, 1674
Arr. Rob MacKillop©

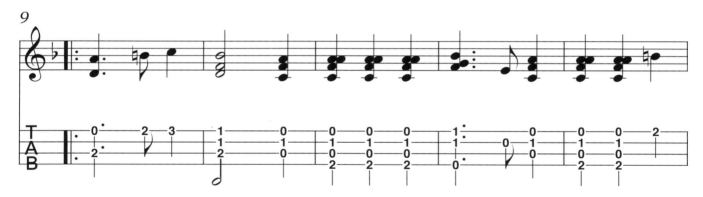

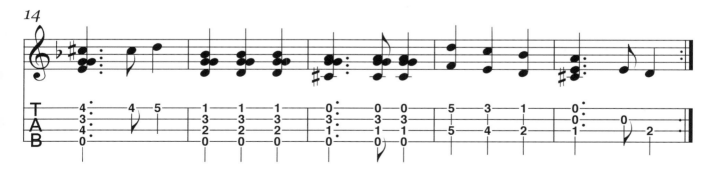

# Matachin

Gaspar Sanz, 1674
Arr. Rob MacKillop©

11

# Rujero

Gaspar Sanz, 1674
Arr. Rob MacKillop©

# Paradetas

Gaspar Sanz, 1674
Arr. Rob MacKillop©

# La esfachata de Napoles

Gaspar Sanz, 1674
Arr. Rob MacKillop©

# La Coquina Francesa

Gaspar Sanz, 1674
Arr. Rob MacKillop©

# La minina de Portugal

Gaspar Sanz, 1674
Arr. Rob MacKillop©

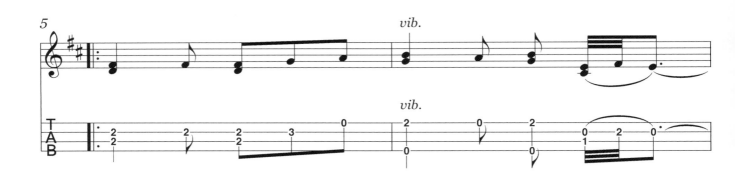

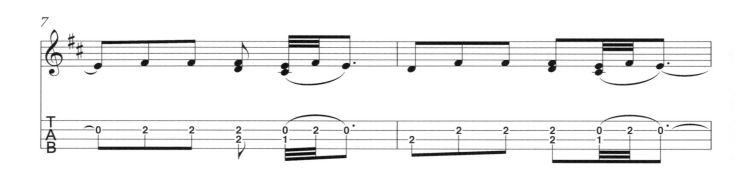

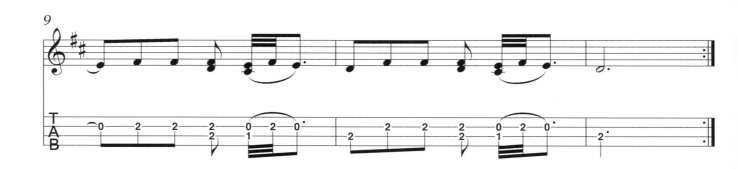

# La miñona de Cataluña

Gaspar Sanz, 1674
Arr. Rob MacKillop©

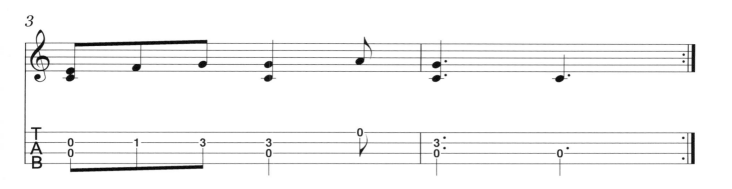

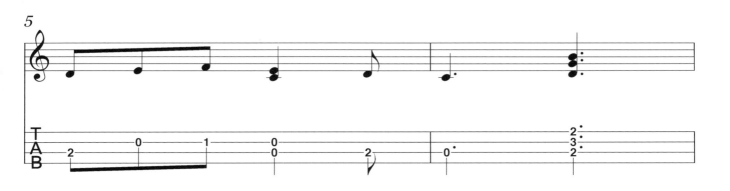

Strum to end...

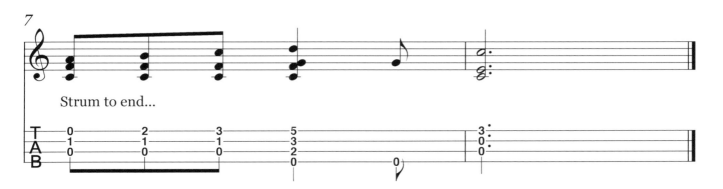

# Lantururu

Gaspar Sanz, 1674
Arr. Rob MacKillop©

18

# Españoleta

Gaspar Sanz, 1674
Arr. Rob MacKillop©

# Jácaras

Gaspar Sanz, 1674
Arr. Rob MacKillop©

21

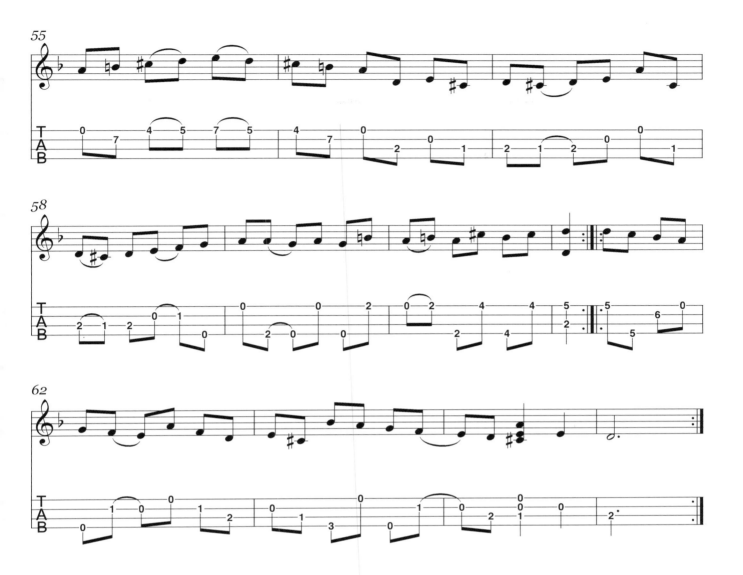

# Folías

Gaspar Sanz, 1674
Arr. Rob MacKillop©

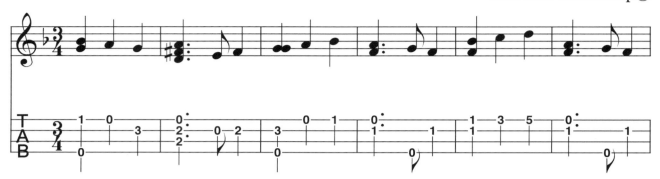

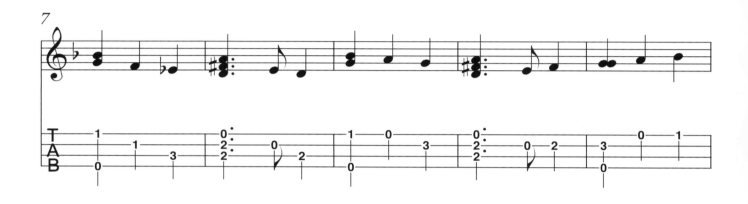

This page has been deliberately left blank

# Pasacalle in Dm

Gaspar Sanz, 1674
Arr. Rob MacKillop©

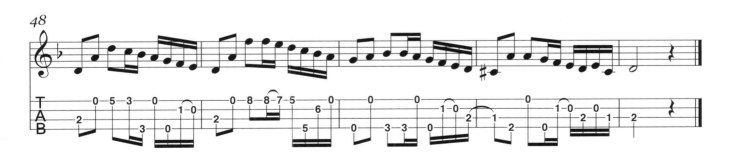

# Canarios

Gaspar Sanz
Arr. Rob MacKillop©

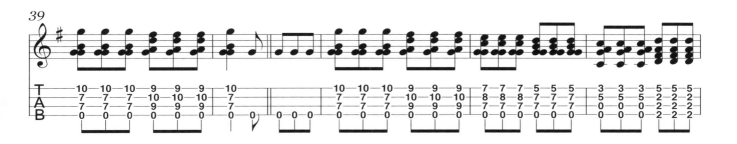

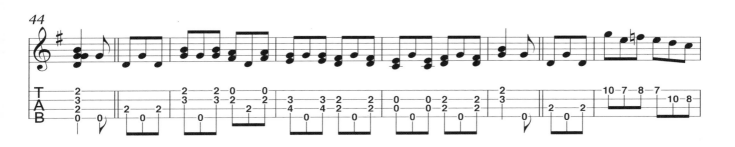

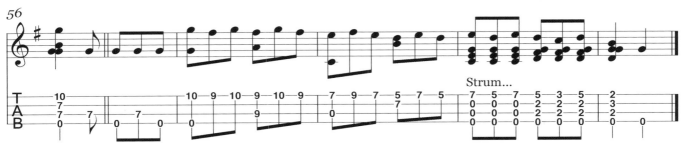

# Alemanda la preciosa

Gaspar Sanz, 1674
Arr. Rob MacKillop©

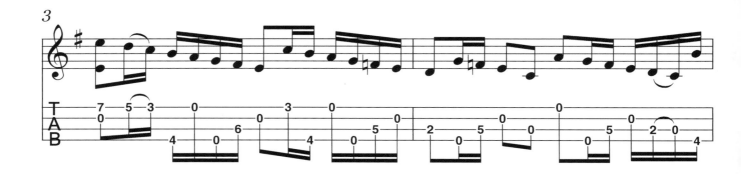

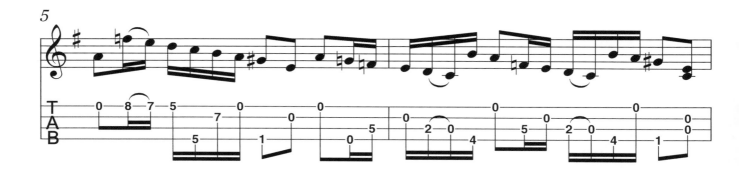

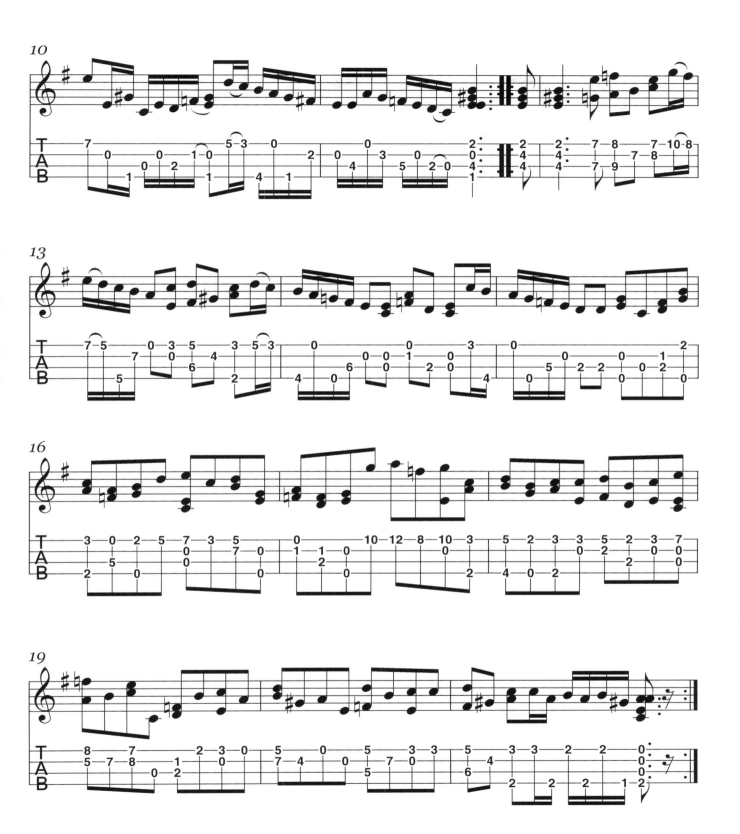

# Coriente

Gaspar Sanz, 1674
Arr. Rob MacKillop©

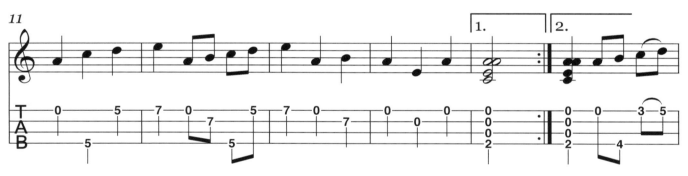

# Fuga

Gaspar Sanz, 1674
Arr. Rob MacKillop©

# Rob MacKillop

Rob MacKillop has recorded eight CDs of historical music, three of which reached the Number One position in the Scottish Classical Music Chart. In 2001 he was awarded a Churchill Fellowship for his research into medieval Scottish music, which led him to studying with Sufi musicians in Istanbul and Morocco. He broadcast an entire solo concert on BBC Radio 3 from John Smith's Square, London.

He has presented academic papers at conferences in Portugal and Germany, and has been published many times. Rob has been active in both historical and contemporary music.

Three of Scotland's leading contemporary composers have written works for him, and he also composes new works himself. In 2004 he was Composer in Residence for Morgan Academy in Dundee, and in 2001 was Musician in Residence for Madras College in St Andrews. He created and Directed the Dundee Summer Music Festival.

He worked as a Reader of schools literature for Oxford University Press, and as a reviewer for *Music Teacher*. He has also been Lecturer in Scottish Musical History at Aberdeen University, Dundee University, and at the Royal Scottish Academy of Music and Drama, and for five years worked as Musician In Residence to Queen Margaret University in Edinburgh. He has been a regular article writer for BMG magazine.

Rob plays banjo, guitar and ukulele with gut strings, plucking the strings with the flesh of his fingers, not the nails. This produces a warm and intimate sound, reminiscent of the old lute players.

robmackillop.net

Checkout www.MelBay.com for more editions by Rob MacKillop

Made in the USA
Coppell, TX
07 March 2020